The happy kangaroo song

1  **Listen and sing.**

2 **Ask your partner:** What's your name? How are you?

English all around

1. There are many English words in the picture.
Look and say: I can see …

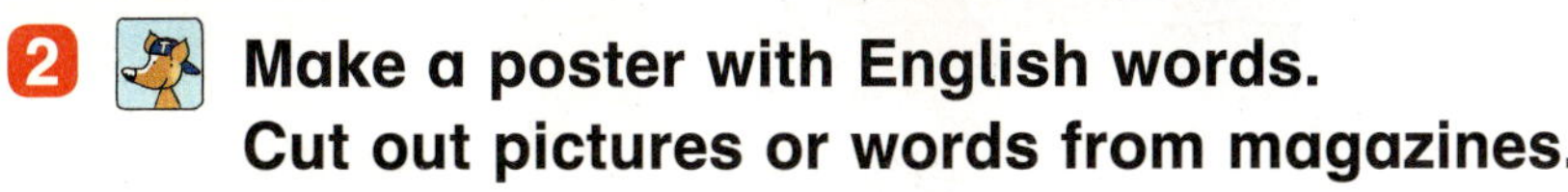

2 Make a poster with English words.
Cut out pictures or words from magazines.

Group the words (sports, food, drinks, …).

Mr Blue and Mrs Yellow

1 🎧 **Listen and point.**

2 💬 **What colour is it?**

3 👦👧 **Act out the story with a partner.**

Sally's rhyme

1  **Listen, say the rhyme and do the actions.**

2 **Learn the rhyme.**

In class

1 Listen and point.

2 **What school things have you got?**
Tell your partner: I've got a ...

Make your own picture dictionary.
Draw and write.

     CD 1.14

School in England

1 💬 **Talk about the photos.**

in class

pupils in school uniform

lunchtime

a lollipop lady

2   **Listen and read.**

Hello, my name is Ella. I'm 9.
I go to Westminster School. I'm in class 3c.
My teacher is Mrs Black.
My school uniform is red and white.
School starts at 9 o'clock in the morning
and ends at 4 o'clock in the afternoon.
My favourite subjects are music and sports.
What about you?

3   **What about your school day? Do a presentation.**

Head and shoulders

1 Sing the song and do the actions.

2 Sing the song faster and faster.

3 Sing and drop the word [head].
Sing again and drop the words [head] and [shoulders] ...

Ouch!

1 **Read the comic.**

Snakes and ladders

1 It's your turn. Play the game and do the actions.

Roll the dice. Do the actions.

 Correct action 🙂 : Go up the ladder.

Wrong action 🙁 : Go down the snake.

Sally's hotspot:

Correct action 🙂 : Roll the dice again.

Wrong action 🙁 : Go back to the start.

3 Touch your head. 

8 Bend your knees. 

16 Sing: Head and shoulders …

19 Wash your hands. 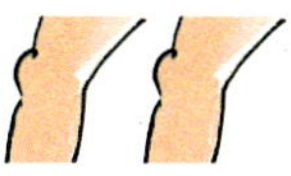

24 Count your fingers. 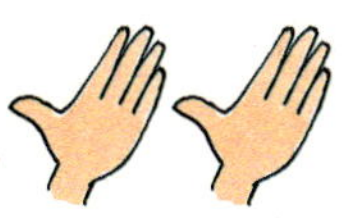

27 Shake your feet. 

29 Stretch your arms. 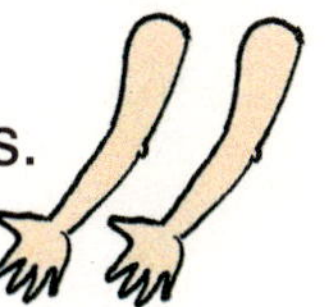

33 Point to your eyes. 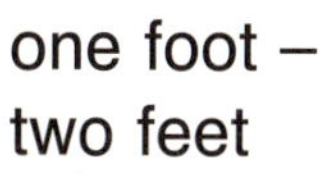

43 Touch your ears. 

48 Stretch your legs. 

52 Brush your hair. 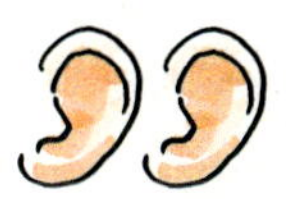

58 Say: Good morning!

59 Point to your nose. 

62 Shake your body. 

Monster, monster how do you feel?

I'm happy
because my hair is cool.

I'm angry
because a dog ate my chocolate.

I'm scared
because a spider is in my shoe.

I'm sad
because my favourite T-shirt
is too small.

I'm tired
because I chased a ghost all night.

 **Listen and read.**

Tim's wish list

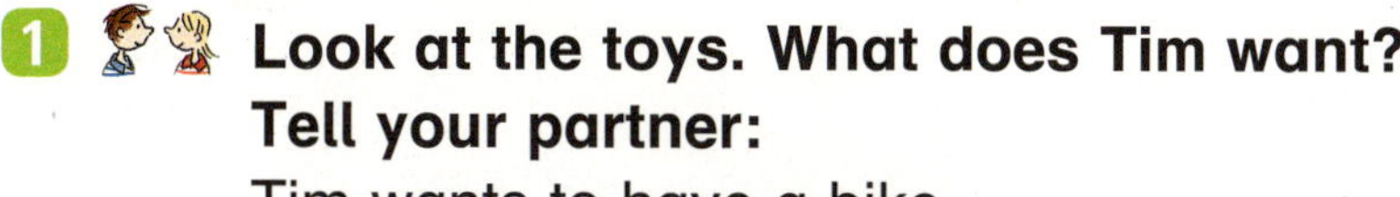

1. Look at the toys. What does Tim want?
Tell your partner:
Tim wants to have a bike …

2. **Ask your partner:** How much is the …?

3. **Make a wish list for your class and discuss.**
We want to have …

I want –
Tim want**s**

The fish who could wish

In the deep blue sea, in the deep of the blue,
swam a fish who could wish, and each wish would come true.

He wished for a castle.

He wished for a car.

He wished for a horse and a Spanish guitar.

One day, just for fun, that silly old fish,
wished the silliest, silliest wish he could wish.

That silly old fish wished he could be
just like all the other fish in the sea.

But wishing was something other fish could not do.
So that was his very last wish that came true.

1 **Listen and point.**

2 **Look at the pictures.**
Tell the story to your partner.

Sally in the snow

1  **Listen and point.**

2 💬 **Look and say:** Sally put**s** on her …
Sally take**s** off her …

3 **Do the clothes rally.**

What's the weather like?

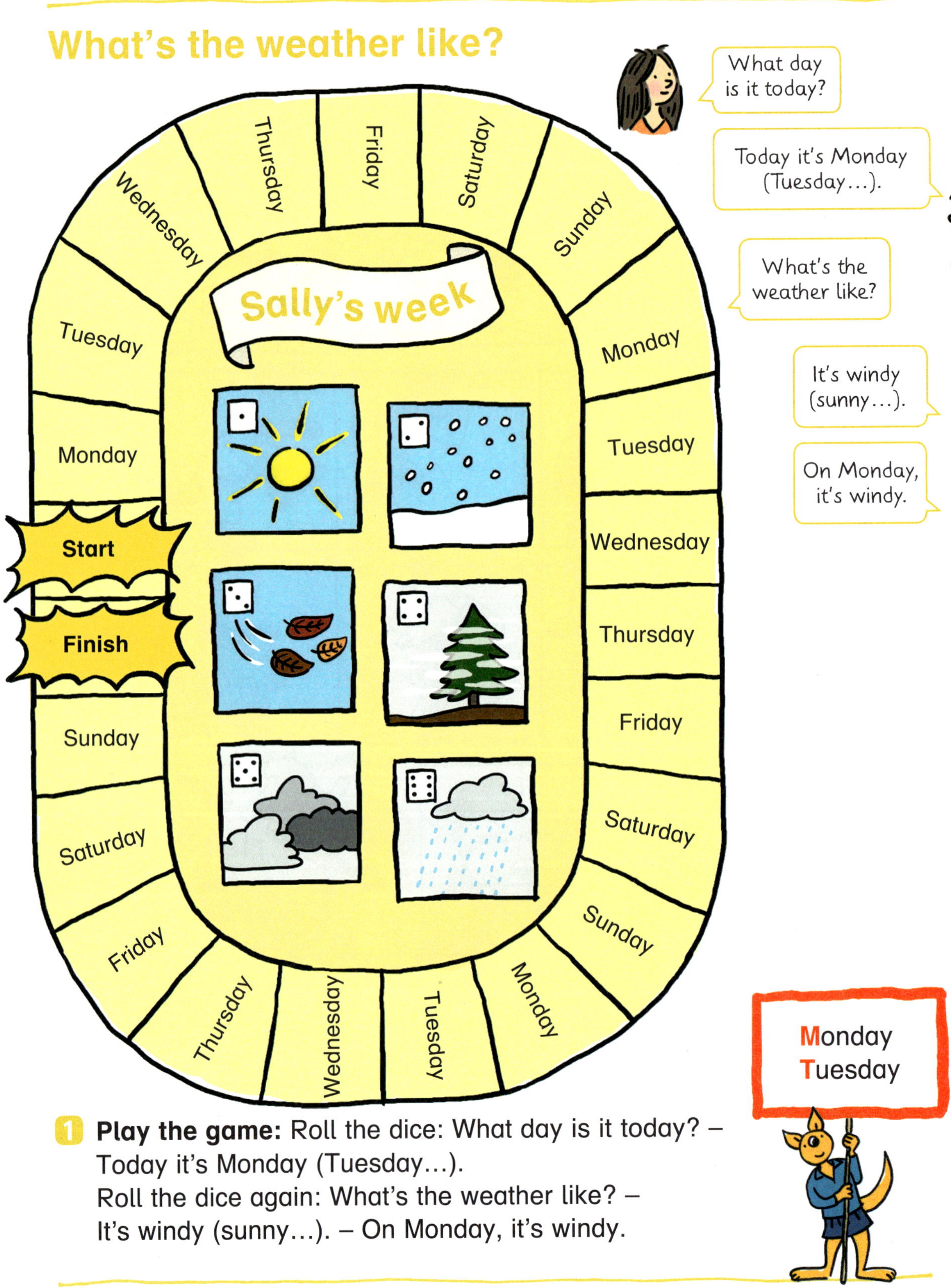

1 **Play the game:** Roll the dice: What day is it today? –
Today it's Monday (Tuesday…).
Roll the dice again: What's the weather like? –
It's windy (sunny…). – On Monday, it's windy.

The wind and the sun

1   **Look at the picture. What can you see?**

2   **Listen to the story. Tell it to your partner.**

3   **Act out the story in your group.**

The weather forecast

1 Talk about the picture.

2 What's the weather like? Listen, point and tell.

3 What's the weather like in Paris, in Hamburg …?
Look in a newspaper or on the Internet.
Make a weather forecast in your group
and do a presentation.

⭐ Make a weather chart for one week.

Presentation tips:
• Speak loudly and clearly.
• Look at the class.
• Show pictures.

Happy birthday

1. Make a birthday calendar.

2. Talk about Emily's birthday party.

3. How do you celebrate your birthday?
   Tell your class.

4. Write a birthday invitation.

Keith Haring

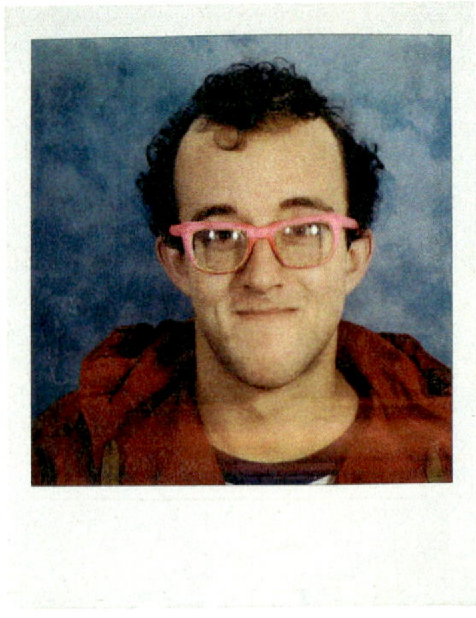

the artist

"Best buddies"

"Football"

"Group"

1 💬 **Look at the pictures.
Describe the colours and actions.**

group work

presentation

"Dancing in the sun"

"Friends"

2  **Make a picture about friends:**
1. Cut out different figures.
2. Glue them on coloured paper.
3. Trace your figures with a black pen.

My family

my mum and dad

My brother Tim
is 9 years old!

my grandma and grandpa

Can you find my grandma
and grandpa?

This is my aunt.
Her name is
Helen.

Can you find my mum
and Tim?

How old is Susan?

1 **Look and point.**

2 **What about your family? Tell.**

What is it?

tea, coke, orange juice, coffee, hot chocolate, milk

1 Look and guess.

At the drinks stand

2 Look and read.

3 Make your own drinks stand. Act out the scene.

4 Make a poster about drinks.

The magic trick

1 Do the trick.

2 Can you do a magic trick?
Show your class.

My favourite breakfast

everyday breakfast

traditional cooked breakfast

1 **Look and speak.**

2 **Ask your partner.**

3 **What do you have for breakfast?**
For breakfast, I have …

4 **Do the breakfast rally.**

At the ice cream stand

1 Listen and speak.

2 **Ask your partner:** What's your favourite ice cream?

⭐ **Find more nouns ending with y. Build the plural.**

Let's make a smoothie

1 Look and read.

This is what you need.

Wash the strawberries.

Peel the bananas.

Cut the fruit.

Put them into the jug.

Add water or milk.

Mix it.

Pour the smoothie
into your glass.

Enjoy!

2  Make your own smoothie.

Little dog lost

1 Listen. Where is Bobby?

These pets have new homes

Jack and Mr Tailor

Tippy and Mrs Davis

Rocky and Sammy Baker

Hopsy and Sophie Miller

Molly and Kevin Fisher

Fred and Alice Smith

Charlie and Mrs Cooper

1 Listen, look and speak.

2 Make a missing pet report.

3 Act it out with your partner.

100 little kangaroos are sitting on Big Ben

100 little kangaroos are sitting on Big Ben.
10 of them just jump away. How many are there then?

90 little kangaroos are sitting on Big Ben.
10 of them just jump away. How many are there then?

80 little kangaroos are sitting on Big Ben.
10 of them just jump away. How many are there then?

70 little kangaroos are sitting on Big Ben.
10 of them just jump away. How many are there then?
…

1 **Listen and sing.**

2 **Sing the song faster and faster.**

twenty, thirty,
forty, …

Let's go to London!

the Royal Family

guards

Buckingham Palace

Tower Bridge

the London Eye

Big Ben

1 Look at the photos.

2 Make a poster about London sights.

Clumsy the dog

1 **Listen to the story.**

2 **Read the story.**

Alphabet rhyme

A B C D E F G,
on the farm there is a bee.

H I J K L M N,
it lands directly on a hen.

O P Q R S T U,
and asks her friendly:
"How are you?"

V W X Y Z,
"I'm fine, but please,
get off my head."

1   **Listen and point.**

2 **Read the rhyme.**

3 **Do the animal rally.**

On the beach

1. 💬 **Look and speak. How many seashells can you find?**

2. **Create your own summer exhibition in groups.
Use your dictionary. Present it to your class.**

Robin Hood's game

1 Play the game.

Robin Hood
Look!
The sheriff is coming.
Go to 16.
Wave to the farmer.
Go to 37.
You want to
have breakfast
on the farm.
Miss a turn.
Hide
behind
the tree.
Go to 19.
Drink some milk.
Go to 34.
Look at
the castle.
Roll the dice again.
Give money to the poor.
Go to 31.
FINISH

Rush hour

The ghost

I saw a ghost.
He saw me, too.
I waved at him.
But he said "Boo!".

Tongue twister

Two witches are watching two watches.
Which witch is watching which watch?

1 Look and read.
Can you say the tongue twister?

⭐ Choose a witch and describe her to your partner.

It's Halloween

1 **Listen to the song.**

2 **Listen to the story.**

Act out the story.

Christmas Eve

1 **Look and find these Christmas things:**
mistletoe, Christmas tree, stockings, Christmas cards, presents

2 **Listen to the story.**

3 **How do you celebrate Christmas?**

I hear them

1. **Listen to the song.**

2. **Sing the song.**

3. **Act out the song.**

4. **Make a Christmas card.**

Make your own Christmas stocking

You need:
thick brown paper, a pencil,
scissors, glue, a hole punch,
wool, felt tips or wax crayons
and coloured paper

1

Draw a large stocking
on the thick brown paper.
Cut out two copies of the stocking.

3

Glue the two stockings
together around the edges.
Leave the top open.

4

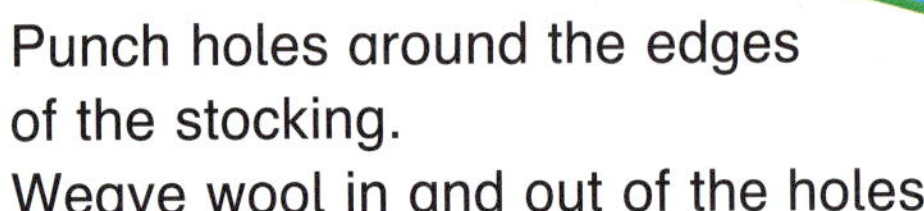

Punch holes around the edges
of the stocking.
Weave wool in and out of the holes.

6

Leave a loop of wool
at one end.
Tie it into a knot.
Decorate your stocking.

 **Look and read.**

2  **Create your own stocking.**

Describe your stocking.

Valentine's cards

1 **Read the comic.**

2 **Read the rhymes. What's your favourite rhyme?**

Jingle, jangle,
silver bangle,
you look fit
from every angle.

Candy is sweet,
this is true,
but for my Valentine
I'll choose you.

I like you!
Be my Valentine!

Roses are red,
violets are blue,
sugar is sweet
and so are you!

3  **Make your own Valentine's card.**

Edgar's Easter eggs

1 Listen to the story. Act it out.

2 Where are the Easter eggs? Look and tell.

3 Look and read.

You need:
a toilet roll, white paper, pink paper,
glue, scissors, felt tips or coloured pencils,
pipe cleaners

Cover the toilet roll
with white paper.

Draw a bunny face
on it.

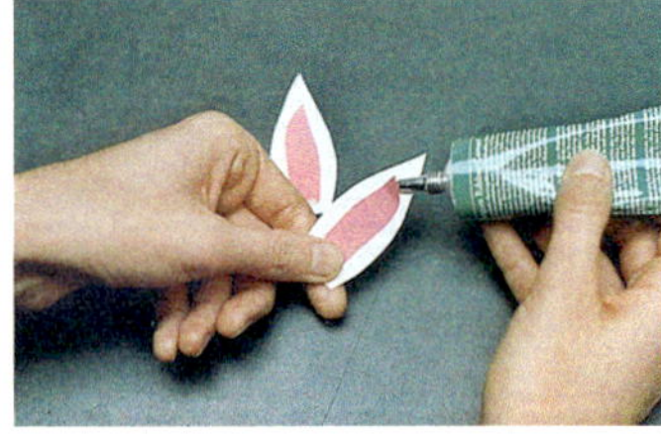

Cut out two ears from the
white paper and the centres
from the pink paper.

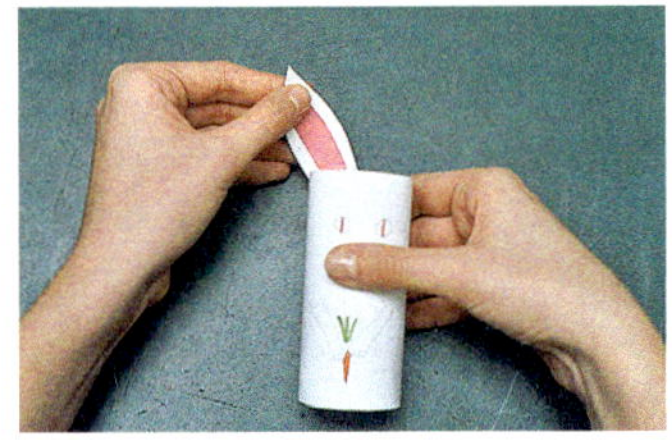

Glue on the ears.

Glue on the
pipe cleaners.

4 Make your own Easter egg cup.

Hello   Hallo

boy   Junge
girl   Mädchen
children   Kinder

basketball   Basketball
computer game   Computerspiel
inline skating   Inlineskaten
singing   Singen
skateboard   Skateboard
tennis   Tennis

Hello./Hi.   Hallo.

Good morning.   Guten Morgen.

How are you? – I'm fine, thanks.
Wie geht es dir? – Danke, gut.

What's your name? – My name is …
Wie heißt du? – Ich heiße …

What do you like? –
I like … And you?
Was magst du? –
Ich mag … Und du?

I can see (a) …   Ich sehe (ein/e) …

Colours and numbers
Farben und Zahlen

black   schwarz
blue   blau
brown   braun
green   grün
grey   grau
orange   orange
pink   rosa, pink
purple   lila
red   rot

white   weiß
yellow   gelb

one   eins
two   zwei
three   drei
four   vier
five   fünf
six   sechs
seven   sieben
eight   acht
nine   neun
ten   zehn

What colour is it? –
It's green (blue …).
Welche Farbe hat es? –
Es ist grün (blau …).

What's your telephone number? –
My telephone number is …
Wie lautet deine Telefonnummer? –
Meine Telefonnummer ist …

At school   In der Schule

(black)board   Tafel
book   Buch
class   Klasse
classroom   Klassenzimmer
computer   Computer
folder   Ordner
glue stick   Klebestift
lollipop lady   Schülerlotsin
pen   Füller
pencil   Bleistift
pencil case   Federmäppchen
pencil sharpener   Spitzer
pupil   Schüler, Schülerin

rubber   Radiergummi
ruler   Lineal
school   Schule
schoolbag   Schultasche
school things   Schulsachen
school uniform   Schuluniform
(a pair of) scissors   eine Schere
teacher   Lehrer, Lehrerin

in   in
on   auf
under   unter

I've got a …   Ich habe ein(e, en) …

I go to Westminster School.
Ich gehe in die Westminster-Schule.

I'm in class 3c.
Ich bin in der Klasse 3c.

My teacher is Mrs/Mr …
Meine Lehrerin / Mein Lehrer
heißt Frau/Herr …

 ## Body and feelings
Körper und Gefühle

arm   Arm
body   Körper
ear   Ohr
eye   Auge
face   Gesicht
finger   Finger
foot – feet   Fuß – Füße
hair   Haar
hand   Hand
head   Kopf
knee   Knie
leg   Bein
mouth   Mund

nose   Nase
shoulder   Schulter
toe   Zeh
tooth – teeth   Zahn – Zähne

angry   zornig
fine   gut
happy   glücklich
sad   traurig
scared   verängstigt, erschrocken
tired   müde

How do you feel? – I'm happy/sad …
I feel …
Wie fühlst du dich? – Ich bin
glücklich/traurig …

I'm okay.   Mir geht's ganz gut.

 ## Toys   Spielzeug

big   groß
car   Auto
castle   Burg, Schloss
children   Kinder
computer game   Computerspiel
doll   Puppe
fish   Fisch
football   Fußball
guitar   Gitarre
helicopter   Hubschrauber
helmet   Helm
horse   Pferd
bike   Fahrrad
racing car   Rennauto
small   klein
spaceship   Raumschiff
teddy bear   Teddybär
(to) want   wollen
(to) wish (for)   sich wünschen

eleven   elf
twelve   zwölf
thirteen   dreizehn
fourteen   vierzehn
fifteen   fünfzehn
sixteen   sechzehn
seventeen   siebzehn
eighteen   achtzehn
nineteen   neunzehn
twenty   zwanzig

British   britisch
money   Geld
penny – pence (p)   Penny – Pence
pound (£)   Pfund

How much is the …? –
The … is … pounds.
Wie viel kostet der (die, das) …? –
Der (die, das) … kostet … Pfund.

How much is it? – It's … pounds.   Wie
viel kostet das? – Das macht … Pfund.

Tim/Susan wants …
Tim/Susan möchte …

Clothes   Kleidung

boots   Stiefel
cap   Kappe
coat   Mantel
dress   Kleid
gloves   Handschuhe
jacket   Jacke
(a pair of) jeans   eine Jeans
pullover   Pullover
(to) put on   anziehen
scarf   Schal
shirt   Hemd

shoes   Schuhe
(a pair of) shorts
eine kurze Hose, Shorts
skirt   Rock
socks   Socken
(to) take off   ausziehen
(a pair of) trousers   eine Hose
T-shirt   T-Shirt
(to) wear   tragen, anhaben
woolly hat   Mütze

For my holidays, I pack …
Für meine Ferien packe ich … ein.

Sally puts on her … / takes off her …
Sally zieht ihr(e, en) … an/aus.

Weather and days
Wetter und Tage

Monday   Montag
Tuesday   Dienstag
Wednesday   Mittwoch
Thursday   Donnerstag
Friday   Freitag
Saturday   Samstag
Sunday   Sonntag
day   Tag
week   Woche

cloud/y   Wolke/wolkig
cold   kalt
fog/gy   Nebel/neblig
hot   heiß
rain/y   Regen/regnerisch
snow/y   Schnee/verschneit
sun/ny   Sonne/sonnig
weather forecast   Wettervorhersage
wind/y   Wind/windig

When can we meet? – We can meet on Monday (Tuesday …).   Wann können wir uns treffen? – Wir können uns am Montag (Dienstag …) treffen.

What day is it today? – Today it's Monday. (Tuesday ...).   Welchen Tag haben wir heute? – Es ist Montag (Dienstag ...).

What's the weather like? – It's windy (sunny …).   Wie ist das Wetter? – Es ist windig (sonnig …).

On Monday, it's sunny.
Am Montag ist es sonnig.

Around the year
Rund ums Jahr

January   Januar
February   Februar
March   März
April   April
May   Mai
June   Juni
July   Juli
August   August
September   September
October   Oktober
November   November
December   Dezember
month   Monat

spring   Frühling
summer   Sommer
autumn   Herbst
winter   Winter
season   Jahreszeit

balloon   Ballon
birthday   Geburtstag
cake   Torte, Kuchen
calendar   Kalender
candle   Kerze
card   Karte
crown   Krone
guest   Gast
invitation   Einladung
party   Party, Feier
present   Geschenk

When's your birthday? –
My birthday is in …
Wann ist dein Geburtstag? –
Mein Geburtstag ist im …

Happy birthday!
Alles Gute zum Geburtstag!

How old are you? – I'm eight (years old).
Wie alt bist du? –
Ich bin acht (Jahre alt).

Family and friends
Familie und Freunde

aunt   Tante
boy   Junge
brother   Bruder
family   Familie
father/dad   Vater/Papa
friend   Freund(in)
girl   Mädchen
grandfather/grandpa   Großvater/Opa
grandmother/grandma
Großmutter/Oma
mother/mum   Mutter/Mama
sister   Schwester
uncle   Onkel

My best friend is ...
Mein(e) beste(r) Freund(in) ist …

He/She is … years old.
Er/Sie ist … Jahre alt.

He/She has got ...   Er/Sie hat …

Have you got brothers or sisters? –
I've got ... / I haven't got ...
Hast du Geschwister? –
Ich habe … / Ich habe keine …

This is my family. /
These are my friends.
Das ist meine Familie. /
Dies sind meine Freunde.

Drinks   Getränke

coffee   Kaffee
coke   Cola
hot chocolate   Kakao
lemonade   Limonade
(a glass of) milk   (ein Glas) Milch
orange juice   Orangensaft
(a cup of) tea   (eine Tasse) Tee
water   Wasser

What drinks do you like? – I like …
Welche Getränke magst du? –
Ich mag …

I like … best.   Am liebsten mag ich …

What drinks don't you like? –
I don't like …
Welche Getränke magst du nicht? –
Ich mag kein(e, en) …

What would you like to drink? –
I'd like …, please.   Was würdest du
gerne trinken? – Ich hätte gerne …, bitte.

Breakfast   Frühstück

bread   Brot
breakfast   Frühstück
butter   Butter
cheese   Käse
cornflakes   Cornflakes
(to) drink   trinken
(to) eat   essen
egg   Ei
ham   Schinken
honey   Honig
jam   Marmelade
roll   Brötchen
toast   Toast

What do you have for breakfast?
Was isst/trinkst du zum Frühstück?

For breakfast, I have …
Zum Frühstück esse/trinke ich …

Do you like …? –
Yes, I do. / No, I don't.
Magst du …? – Ja. / Nein.

Can I have the …, please? –
Here you are.   Kann ich bitte den/die/
das … haben? – Hier, bitte.

Fruit   Obst

apple   Apfel
banana   Banane
cherry   Kirsche
fruit   Frucht, Obst
lemon   Zitrone
melon   Melone
orange   Orange, Apfelsine
pear   Birne

pineapple Ananas	mouse – mice Maus – Mäuse
plum Pflaume	pet Haustier
strawberry Erdbeere	rabbit Kaninchen
tree Baum	tail Schwanz
	tortoise Schildkröte
(to) add hinzufügen	wing Flügel

pineapple   Ananas
plum   Pflaume
strawberry   Erdbeere
tree   Baum

(to) add   hinzufügen
(to) cut   schneiden
ice cream   Eiskrem
ice cream stand   Eisstand
jug   Krug
(to) mix   mischen
(to) peel   schälen
(to) pour   eingießen
(to) put   hineingeben, legen, stellen
scoop   Eiskugel
smoothie   Smoothie, Fruchtshake
(to) wash   waschen

What's your favourite ice cream?
Was ist dein Lieblingseis?

Can I help you?
Kann ich dir/euch/Ihnen helfen?

I'd like … – Here you are.
Ich hätte gerne … – Hier, bitte.

That's … pounds, please. – Thank you.
Das macht bitte … Pfund. – Danke.

Goodbye.   Auf Wiedersehen.

Pets   Haustiere

bird   Vogel
budgie   Wellensittich
cat   Katze
dog   Hund
fish   Fisch(e)
guinea pig   Meerschweinchen
hamster   Hamster

mouse – mice   Maus – Mäuse
pet   Haustier
rabbit   Kaninchen
tail   Schwanz
tortoise   Schildkröte
wing   Flügel

What's your favourite pet?
Was ist dein Lieblingshaustier?

My favourite pet is a …
Mein Lieblingshaustier ist ein(e) …

Its name is …   Es heißt …

Can I help you? – I've lost my pet.
Kann ich dir/euch/Ihnen helfen? – Ich
habe mein Haustier verloren.

What colour is it? – It's black
(brown …).
Welche Farbe hat es? – Es ist
schwarz (braun …).

 **London**   London
England   England
guard   Wache, Wachposten
king   König
(to) move   bewegen, sich bewegen
palace   Palast
prince   Prinz
princess   Prinzessin
queen   Königin
Royal Family   Königsfamilie
sight   Sehenswürdigkeit

I want to be a …   Ich will ein(e) … sein.

I want to see …   Ich will … sehen.

 **Farm animals**
Bauernhoftiere

animal   Tier
barn   Stall
bee   Biene
clumsy   ungeschickt
cow   Kuh
duck   Ente
farm   Bauernhof
farmer   Bauer
goose – geese   Gans – Gänse
hen   Huhn, Henne
horse   Pferd
pig   Schwein
sheep   Schaf, Schafe

What's your favourite animal? –
It's a …
Was ist dein Lieblingstier? –
Es ist ein(e) …

 **Summer**   Sommer

airbed   Luftmatratze
beach   Strand
beach ball   Wasserball
(to) build   bauen
holidays   Ferien
ice cream   Eiskrem
(to) play   spielen
sand   Sand
sandcastle   Sandburg
sea   Meer
seashell   Muschel
(to) snorkel   schnorcheln
suncream   Sonnenkrem
sunglasses   Sonnenbrille
(to) swim   schwimmen
towel   Handtuch

How many … can you see/find? –
I can see/find …
Wie viele … kannst du sehen/finden? –
Ich kann … sehen/finden.

 **Robin Hood**   Robin Hood

arrow   Pfeil
bow   Bogen
castle   Burg, Schloss
(to) catch   fangen
(to) dress up   sich verkleiden
forest   Wald
hat   Hut
(to) play a trick
einen Streich spielen
poor   arm
rich   reich
(to) ride (a horse)
(ein Pferd) reiten
sheriff   Sheriff
(to) shoot   schießen

Help!   Hilfe!

Hands up!   Hände hoch!

 **Happy Halloween**
Fröhliches Halloween

bat   Fledermaus
broom   Besen
costume   Kostüm, Verkleidung
dark   dunkel
door   Tür
ghost   Geist, Gespenst
Halloween   Halloween
hat   Hut
house   Haus
(to) knock   klopfen

monster   Ungeheuer, Monster
moon   Mond
night   Nacht
pumpkin   Kürbis
(to) shake   schütteln
skeleton   Geripppe, Skelett
star   Stern
sweets   Süßigkeiten
witch   Hexe

Happy Halloween!
Fröhliches Halloween!

It's eight (nine …) o'clock.
Es ist acht (neun …) Uhr.

Trick or treat!   Süßes oder Saures!

Merry Christmas
Frohe Weihnachten

bell   Glocke
carrot   Karotte
chimney   Schornstein
Christmas card   Weihnachtskarte
Christmas Eve   Heiligabend,
Weihnachtsabend
Christmas tree   Weihnachtsbaum
Father Christmas   Weihnachtsmann
fireplace   (offener) Kamin
(to) get presents   Geschenke
bekommen
mistletoe   Mistel(zweig)
reindeer   Rentier(e)
sleigh   Schlitten
snowman   Schneemann
stocking   Strumpf

Merry Christmas!   Frohe Weihnachten!

Valentine's Day
Valentinstag

Valentine's Day   Valentinstag

(to) write Valentine's cards
Valentinskarten schreiben

It's Valentine's Day.
Es ist Valentinstag.

I like you.   Ich mag dich.

Happy Easter   Frohe Ostern

basket   Korb
bush   Busch
(to) colour   färben, anmalen
Easter bunny   Osterhase
Easter egg   Osterei
Easter egg cup   Ostereierbecher
fence   Zaun
fun   Spaß
happy   glücklich
(to) hide   verstecken
sad   traurig
(to) share   teilen

behind   hinter
in   in
in front of   vor
on   auf
under   unter

Happy Easter!   Frohe Ostern!

Is the yellow (red …) egg in/on/under
the …?
Ist das gelbe (rote …) Ei in/auf/unter
dem/der …?